Catholicism
in Light of Orthodoxy

CATHOLICISM
IN LIGHT OF ORTHODOXY

Archimandrite George
Abbot of the Holy Monastery of Grigoriou,
Mt. Athos

Translated by Vincent DeWeese

Uncut Mountain Press

CATHOLICISM IN LIGHT OF ORTHODOXY

© 2022
Uncut Mountain Press

uncutmountainpress.com

We are especially grateful to Archimandrite Christopher and the brotherhood of the Holy Monastery of Grigoriou on Mt. Athos for the blessing and permission to translate and publish this small but important essay by their ever-memorable elder, Abbot George.

Cover Artwork: Holy Monastery of Grigoriou (above) and Vatican City (below). Design by George Weis.

Scriptural quotations are primarily taken from the King James Version.

Library of Congress Cataloging-in-Publication Data

Archimandrite George, Abbot of the Holy Monastery of Grigoriou.
Catholicism in Light of Orthodoxy—1st ed.
Written by Elder George of Grigoriou (+ June 8, 2014)
Translated by Vincent DeWeese.
Edited by Karen Evans.

ISBN: 978-1-63941-015-6

I. Orthodox Christianity
II. Orthodox Christian Ecclesiology

Translator's Note

As with all works of translation, there are a number of places where the translator has felt the need to change the word order or make more substantial changes to the syntax of sentences in order to conform to good English style. He hopes that in doing so he has not in any way distorted the words of the holy Elder of most blessed memory. It must also be noted that every instance where Elder George has used a Greek source and an English edition was already readily available, the English edition has been substituted for the original Greek source. In cases where an English edition was unavailable, the translator has left the original Greek citation. All biblical citations are from the King James Version.

TABLE OF CONTENTS

the faith which was once delivered unto the saints
St. Jude, Brother of the Lord

INTRODUCTION

The Main Differences

After the ascension of the new Pope, Benedict XVI, to the throne of Rome, it was announced that theological dialogue between Orthodoxy and Roman Catholicism which had been interrupted because of the problem of Uniatism in July of 2000 would resume. There have been many assessments of the stance which the new Pontiff would take concerning the serious theological problems which exist and impede the restoration of ecclesiastical unity.

Independently from these assessments, we Orthodox see the restoration of ecclesiastical unity as the return of the Roman Catholics to the "the faith which was once delivered unto the saints,"[1] which they departed from with the heretical dogmas of papal primacy of authority, papal infallibility, the Filioque, created Grace, and others.

In order to be aware of what we expect from the Dialogue, which it seems will begin again, we are publishing with some modifications a homily which we had given in 1998 with the theme: the basic differences between the Orthodox Churches and Roman Catholicism. The homily was delivered at the invitation of the local Metropolitan, in a provincial city where

---

1 Jude 3:3

they had been presented with outbreaks of proselytism against the Orthodox on the part of Roman Catholics.[2]

One of the characteristics of our pluralistic age is the attempt of rapprochement between different peoples and civilizations. Toward this end, empowered representatives of the different Christian confessions and religions come together at certain intervals to conduct official and unofficial dialogues. To make the realization of these dialogues possible in the beginning they seek the discovery of some points of commonality between the dialoguing parties. For this reason, the enumeration of the differences between our holy Orthodox faith and Roman Catholicism may be considered strange at the present historical juncture.

However, a superficial ecumenism which ignores the differences takes us further away from rather than bringing us closer to union. Concerning this superficial ecumenism, Father Dimitru Staniloae writes: "Every now and then an easy enthusiasm from a great desire for union is created which believes that it can with its affective warmth melt down reality and to shape it again without difficulty. Furthermore, a diplomatic compromising mindset is created which thinks that it can reconcile with mutual concessions of dogmatic positions or more generally conditions, which keep the churches separated. These two ways with which the reality is dealt with—or left unconsidered—show a certain elasticity or relativism of the value which is attributed to the defined articles of faith of the churches. This relativism reflects perhaps the very low importance, which certain Christian groups—as a whole or certain people from their circles—give to these articles of faith. They suggest the above from enthusiasm or a diplomatic mindset, these exchanges and

---

2 See periodical, MAPTΥΡIA, Ἰ. Μητροπόλεως Κυδωνίας και Ἀποκορώνου, τεύχος 192, January, February 1998, Chania, Crete [Greek].

compromises, precisely because they do not have anything to lose with what they suggest. These compromises however present a great danger for Churches where the corresponding articles have importance of the first order. For these Churches, such suggestions of exchange and compromise are equivalent to overt attacks."[3]

There exists another reason which requires us to know the differences: the preservation in a state of vigilance of the dogmatic consciousness of the Orthodox.

We live in an age of confusion, inter-Christian and inter-religious syncretism and promotion of the so-called "New Age." The faithful of our Church are not left unaffected.

Recently, a professor at the University of Athens wrote that he can just as easily light a candle before the icon of the Panagia as before the statue of one of the gods of Hinduism.

It is the bounden pastoral duty of the Shepherds of our Church to confess the Orthodox Faith without compromises, when they dialogue with the heterodox, but also to teach it to the Orthodox people, especially where it is muddled by ignorance of the differences with the other dogmas and religions. Even more so must they teach the Faith and demonstrate the differences in regions where direct or indirect proselytism is being used. The counsel of the great Apostle Paul to the bishops and presbyters of the Church echoes still today: "Take heed therefore unto yourselves, and to all the flock, over the which the Holy Ghost hath made you overseers, to feed the church of God, which he hath purchased with his own blood."[4]

Let us examine the most important differences.

---

3 Dimitru Staniloae, *Concerning an Orthodox Ecumenism*, published ΑΘΩΣ, Piraeus 1976, pp. 19-20. [Greek].

4 Acts 20:28.

St. Nikodemos the Hagiorite

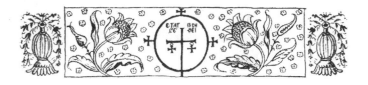

CHAPTER 1

The Vatican State

The Vatican is the center of the administrative-bureaucratic system of Roman Catholicism—of the Papal Church and of the Papal state. The Pope is the leader of the "Roman Catholic Church" and simultaneously the leader of the Vatican state which has government ministers, an economy, in older times an army, and today a police force, diplomacy and whatever else constitutes a state.

We all know how many long and bloody wars happened in the past on account of the Popes, and indeed during the Investiture Controversy which began with Pope Gregory VII in 1075 and which lasted for 200 years. The aim of these wars was the security but also the expansion of the Vatican state. Even today although territorially reduced, the Vatican still actively promotes its own interests, with the result that other peoples and indeed the Orthodox are struck as recently as the war of the Croatians and Muslims against the Orthodox Serbs.

The Pope in various countries is represented by a Nuncio who is his eyes and ears. In Athens there exists the Latin Archbishop, the Uniate Bishop and the Nuncio—three representatives of the Pope. The Pope's papocaesarist claims are summarized characteristically in what was said by Pope Innocent IV (1198-1216), the greatest of the medieval Popes, in his enthronement speech: "The one having the bride is the bridegroom. But the bride (the Church) is not married with empty hands, but she brings to me an incomparable and invaluable dowry, namely the fullness of spiritual goods, the amplitude of worldly goods, and the splendor and abundance of both… As a symbol of the worldly goods she gives to me the Crown, and the Miter for the priesthood, the Crown for kingship and she renders me representative of Him upon Whose garment and thigh it was written: the King of Kings and Lord of Lords."[1] According to the western tradition, the emperor was obliged to keep the bridle and stirrup of the papal horse in official meetings demonstrating his submission to the Pope.

The coexistence in the same person of ecclesiastical and political authority is, according to the teaching of our Lord and of the Holy Apostles, unacceptable. The saying of our Lord is well-known: "Render to Caesar the things that are Caesar's, and to God the things that are God's."[2] St. Nikodemos of the Holy Mountain characterizes this coexistence as "a mixture unmixable and a freakish monster."[3] It is a sign of the terrible secularization of the Church, the confusion of the two authorities, the spiritual and worldly—of the two kingdoms, of heaven and of those upon the earth. Thus, the Church yields to the second temptation of Christ from the devil when he requested Him to worship him in order to be given authority over all the kingdoms of the world. The Lord then answered him: "Thou shalt worship the Lord thy God, and him only shalt thou serve."[4] Let us remember the

---

1 Migne, PL 217, 665AB. See also: Ἀρχιμ. Σπ. Μπιλάλη, Ὀρθοδοξία καὶ Παπισμός, Ἔκδ. Ἀδελφ. «Εὐνίκη», Ἀθῆναι 1988, p. 155 [Greek].

2 Mark 12:17.

3 The Rudder, publ. Β. Πηγοπούλου, Thessaloniki 1982, p. 109 [Greek].

4 Matt. 4:10.

Grand Inquisitor of Dostoevsky. By this unmixable mixture the entire institution of the Church is adversely affected and secularized.

Our difference with the Vatican is important and it will be necessary to discuss it in the coming dialogue. How can the Holy Orthodox Church be united with a Church which is also a State?

Let it be noted here that state authority is one thing while the "economic" undertaking of the temporary mission of the [Ecumenical] Patriarch as "Ethnarch" for the consolation and support of those in the Church who have found themselves in institutional slavery. Our Church in difficult historical periods of slavery and oppression has always charged the Patriarch and the Bishops with the duties of Ethnarch. The Ethnarch however has an absolutely different role from the prime minister or the president of a democracy, which are shouldered with the burden of state power. The Ethnarch is the protector of the persecuted and suffering Orthodox people. It is generally known how important a mission the Ecumenical Patriarchs played as Ethnarchs, not only of the Orthodox Greeks but of all Orthodox peoples throughout the period of the Turkish Yoke, many of whom paid for their role with their blood—tortured and put to death by the Turks such as Saint Gregory V.

Now let us come to the other theological differences.

S AIII T THC

PH ΘΤΙ ΘS GBEAT

St. Photios the Great

CHAPTER 2

The Filioque

A well-known matter is the addition of "and from the Son" to the article concerning the Holy Spirit in the Symbol of Faith (the Nicene Creed). According to their [Latin] teaching, the Holy Spirit proceeds not only from the Father, as our Lord says in the Holy Gospel, but also from the Son. First, Photios the Great, and afterwards many great Fathers such as St. Gregory Palamas, St. Mark Eugenikos, and others condemned this heretical addition with irrefutable arguments.

Photios the Great writes: "The Lord and our God says, 'the Spirit, who proceeds from the Father'; but the fathers of this new impiety, 'the Spirit,' they say, 'who proceeds from the Son'. Who will not shut his ears to this excess of blasphemy? It stands against the Gospels, is set against the Ecumenical Councils, effaces the blessed and holy fathers, Athanasius the Great, Gregory (famed in theology), Basil the Great (the royal garment of the Church), the golden mouth of the world [John Chrysostom] (the sea of wisdom, the truly golden-mouthed). And what do I say to such a one or another? This blasphemy itself and God-fighting voice arms itself against all that is common among the holy prophets, apostles, hierarchs, martyrs and the voices of the same, which belong to the Lord."[1]

In agreement with the teaching of the holy Fathers, this addition is contrary to the Gospel. The Lord explicitly says that the Holy Spirit proceeds from the Father. The Filioque infringes upon the Trinitarian mystery because it introduces dyarchy into the Holy Trinity and rationalizes the supra-rational Mystery, that is to say, it attempts to approach it logically and not through faith.

What Vladimir Lossky has to say on this subject is quite illustrative: "If in the former approach faith seeks understanding, in order to transpose revelation onto the plane of philosophy, in the latter approach understanding seeks the realities of faith, in order to be transformed, by becoming more and more open to the mysteries of revelation. Since the dogma of the Trinity is the keystone of the arch of all theological thought and belongs to the region which the Greek Fathers called *Theologia par excellence*, it is understandable that a divergence in this culminating point, insignificant as it may seem at first sight, should have a decisive importance."[2] It is "a philosophical anthropomorphism having nothing in common with Biblical anthropomorphism."[3] "By the dogma of the Filioque, the God of the philosophers and savants is introduced into the heart of the Living God, taking the place of the *Deus absconditus, qui posuit tenebras latibulum suum*[4]. The unknowable essence of the Father, Son, and Holy Spirit receives positive qualifications. It becomes the object of natural theology: we get 'God in general,' who

---

1 Photios the Great, Epistle 1, 13, 16, PG 102, 728D, 729A.

2 Lossky, Vladimir. *In the Image and Likness of God* (SVS Press: Crestwood, NY, 1976. p. 80.

3 Ibid., p. 86.

4 "The hidden God, who made darkness his hiding place."

could be the god of Descartes, or the god of Leibnitz, or
even perhaps, to some extent, the god of Voltaire and of the
de-Christianized Deists of the eighteenth century."[5]

His All-Holiness the Ecumenical Patriarch, speaking at
the University of Thessaloniki on the 1st of October 1997,
showed the particular importance of the effects of the Filioque on Ecclesiology.[6]

And this is very important, because some Orthodox
Christians and heterodox maintain that the East and West
expressed the same apostolic tradition in different ways
and that this is allegedly the Photianic tradition. Only by
a terrible distortion of history could they formulate such
views and they even attribute these views to Photios the
Great, the confessor of Orthodoxy who strongly censured
the cacodoxy of the Filioque.

---

5 Ibid. p. 88

6 See ΕΠΕΣΚΕΨΑΤΟ ΗΜΑΣ (Πατριαρχικαί επισκέψεις εις την
συμβασιλεύουσαν, 1997-1999-2000), έκδ. Ι. Μητροπόλεως Θεσσαλονίνης,
Θες/νίκη 2000. [Greek].

St. Gregory Palamas

CHAPTER 3

Created Grace

When in the 14th century, the Western monk Barlaam came to Byzantium and preached created Grace of God, the Orthodox faithful with Saint Gregory Palamas confessed that divine Grace is uncreated.

This is also an important difference.

If divine Grace is created, it cannot divinize man. The purpose of the life in Christ, if divine Grace is created, cannot be theosis but ethical improvement. For this reason, the westerners do not speak about theosis as the aim of the life of man, but about ethical perfection—that we ought to become better men, not however gods by grace. As a result, the Church cannot be a communion of theosis, but a foundation affording to men justification in a nominalist and legal manner by means of a created grace. In the final analysis, the very truth of the Church as real theanthropic communion is abolished.

In this case, the Mysteries of the Church are not signs of the presence of God in the Church and of the communion with the uncreated Grace of God, but in some way, "faucets" which the Church opens and out flows created grace, with which men wait to benefit and to be legally justified. Thus, even the Mysteries are interpreted legally and not ecclesiologically. Ascesis also lapses into ethical gymnastics.

The struggling Christian cannot receive experience of the uncreated Grace. He does not behold the uncreated Light of Tabor. And so, according to the divine Palamas, he remains inconsolable and untouched by the Divine Light. He does not participate in the glory, the brightness, and the Kingdom of the Trinitarian God. Thus, theology without experience of the uncreated Light becomes scholastic and discursive. Man remains closed off in the dark prison of the present world without an opening or a foretaste of the coming Kingdom.

Our Orthodox Church with the great Synods of the 14th century approved the teachings of the distinction between the essence and energy of God and concerning His uncreated Energies and the uncreated Light, and established this as her theology. It declared Saint Gregory Palamas as a fixed teacher and luminary of the Church and anathematized those who did not accept his teaching. The papists until this day have not accepted his teaching and a great many fight against St. Gregory Palamas.

It is this important difference which has not been discussed in theological dialogue but by its nature must be discussed. Because, if union were ever to occur, can we believe in uncreated Grace while they believe in created? Let us remember here the word of Saint Gregory the Theologian to the Pneumatomachians: "If the Holy Spirit is not God, let Him first be made God, and then let Him deify me His equal."[1]

The unshaken faith of the Orthodox Church is that the divine Grace is an uncreated energy of the Triadic God and is seen mystically and secretly by the perfect and holy as Taboric Light. This is the experience of the Church as lived by the Saints through the ages.

---

1 St. Gregory the Theologian, Oration 34 "On the Arrival of the Egyptians" <<http://www.newadvent.org/fathers/310234.htm>>.

According to St. Mark of Ephesus, "we affirm, in agreement with the Fathers, that the will and energy of the uncreated and divine nature are uncreated; while they, together with the Latins and Thomas, say that will is identical with nature, but that the divine energy is created, whether it be called divinity, or the divine and immaterial light, or the Holy Spirit, or something else of this nature—and in some fashion, these poor creatures worship the created 'divinity' and the created 'divine light' and the created 'Holy Spirit.'"[2]

Examples and personal witnesses of the contemporary holy elders, such as the blessed Elders Sophrony and Paisios, confirm the truthfulness of his words. The blessed elder Sophrony Sakharov, monk of the Holy Mountain and the founder of the Stavropegial Monastery of the Honorable Forerunner in Essex, England, described his experience of the uncreated Light in the important books which he wrote and lovingly left us as an inheritance.[3]

2 St. Mark (Eugenicus) of Ephesus, "Encyclical to All Orthodox Christians on the Mainland and in the Islands" <<blogs.ancientfaith.com/onbehalfofall/the-encyclical-letterof-mark-of-ephesus/>>.

3 *We Shall See Him As He Is, Saint Silouan, On Prayer*, etc.

St. Justin (Popovich) of Serbia

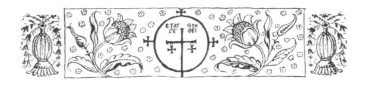

CHAPTER 4

Primacy of Authority & Papal Infallibility

With the teaching of the Filioque, according to which "the Holy Spirit proceeds also from the Son," a dyarchy is introduced into the Holy Trinity which leads to ditheism,[1] and the Holy Spirit is subordinated. This subordination of the Holy Spirit creates a serious void in the Church which someone must fill. One man wanted to do this and this man is the Pope. Thus, the infallibility of the Church through the Holy Spirit is transferred to one 'infallible' man as well as authority over the entire Church.

In order to not do injustice to the Roman Catholic Church, we quote at length a characteristic excerpt from the "Dogmatic Decree Concerning the Church" from the books containing the decisions of the Second Vatican Council, which Roman Catholics consider the 20th Ecumenical Council:[2]

---

1 St. Photios, "Encyclical to all the Eastern archiepiscopal thrones" in Ioannis Karmiris, *Dogmatic and Symbolic Monuments of the Orthodox Catholic Church*, Athens 1960. Vol. 1. P. 323, paragraph 9 [Greek].

2 The Roman Catholics as it is known do not stop at the 7th Ecumenical Council, but they add to them thirteen more. These synods today are for them a great obstacle because, even if they would like to overcome scholasticism and the forensic spirit, they are unable, being bound by the decisions of these synods. The reader of the Catechism of the Catholic Church comes to this conclusion, and it is the most recent

"But the College, or the Body of Bishops, does not have authority, if it is not found in communion with the Bishop of Rome, the successor of Peter and head of the College, because the authority of Primacy remains whole over all the shepherds and the faithful. In reality, the Bishop of Rome with the office as vicar of Christ and shepherd of the entire Church has a full, supreme and worldwide authority within the Church which he can always freely exercise… The Bishop of Rome, as successor of Peter, is the unfailing and visible Head and the foundation of unity, both of the bishops, and even more of the host of the faithful."

We quote also relevant excerpts from the official "Catechism of the Catholic Church":[3]

"The sole Church of Christ [is that] which our Savior, after his Resurrection, entrusted to Peter's pastoral care, commissioning him and the other apostles to extend and rule it.… This Church, constituted and organized as a society in the present world, subsists in (*subsistit in*) the Catholic Church, which is governed by the successor of Peter and by the bishops in communion with him" (816). "'The college of bishops exercises power over the universal Church in a solemn manner in an ecumenical council.' But 'there never is an ecumenical council which is not confirmed or at least recognized as such by Peter's successor'" (884). "'The Roman Pontiff, head of the college of bishops, enjoys this infallibility in virtue of his office, when, as supreme pastor and teacher of all the faithful—who confirms his brethren in the faith he proclaims by a definitive act a doctrine pertaining to faith or morals…'" (891) "In our day, the lawful

official catechism after the Second Vatican Council and reflects its spirit. [Author's note]

3 All Catechism quotations have been taken from the official English translation found on the Vatican website. Paragraph numbers are given in parentheses.

ordination of a bishop requires a special intervention of the Bishop of Rome, because he is the supreme visible bond of the communion of the particular Churches in the one Church and the guarantor of their freedom" (1559).

It is still worthy of attention that the Pope in official texts does not sign as Bishop of Rome but as Bishop of the catholic church or simply with his name, for example, John-Paul II. Obviously, he considers himself a Super-bishop (Ὑπερεπίσκοπον) or as Bishop of Bishops.

The dogma of 'infallibility' was recognized and defined further by the Second Vatican Council: "This religious submission of mind and will must be shown according in a special way to the authentic magisterium of the Roman Pontiff even when he is not speaking *ex cathedra*."[4]

This shows how infallibility was extended to every decision of the Pope. That is to say, whereas with the First Vatican Council, only those decisions of the Pope which were *ex cathedra* and with the use of the term *definimus* (we define) were infallible, the Second Vatican Council ruled that the Pope is infallible not only when he rules officially as Pope but anytime he rules.

It is still clear from the above that the ecumenical synod becomes an advisory organization for the Pope. Infallibility in the Roman Catholic Church does not belong to the ecumenical council but to the Pope. Who, however, confirmed the Pope infallible? The fallible synod?

In this manner, the conciliar principle handed down from the holy Apostles is exchanged for the papocentric principle. The "infallible" Pope becomes the center and source of unity of the Church which means that the Church has need of a man in order to preserve her unity. Thus, the place of Christ and the Holy Spirit is pushed aside and den-

---

4 Lumen Gentium, 25a.

igrated. And further, with the transfer of infallibility from
the Holy Spirit to the person of the Pope, the eschatological
perspective of the Church within history is limited and
becomes secularized.

The Orthodox read these above decisions with deep
sorrow, but also with holy indignation. We consider them
blasphemy against the Holy Spirit. Hence, we understand
the strict but also compassionate words of blessed Father
Justin Popović: "In the history of mankind, there are three
main falls: of Adam, of Judas, and of the Pope."[5]

The Orthodox Church used similar strict language
such as that of Father Justin Popović through the centuries.
To the papal claims concerning primacy of authority and
infallibility, the Orthodox have always responded with the
Orthodox Ecclesiology.

According to Metrophanes Kritopoulos, Patriach of
Alexandria: "Never was it heard that a man mortal and
guilty of a myriad of sins was called head of the Church.
For being a man, he is subject to death. Insofar as another
will be picked to be his successor, so much of the time by
necessity the Church will be without a head. But just as a
body without a head is able neither to stand in the force of
the wind, nor is it possible for the Church without an atten-
tive head to remain upon the rock. Accordingly the Church
has need of an immortal head, which is always living and
active, in the same way as the head of the body… For these
reasons, the head of the Catholic Church is the Lord Jesus
Christ, He who is the head of all, by whom the whole body
is put together."

And according to Dositheos of Jerusalem, in his well-
known "Confession" during the Turkish yoke (1672): "Since
a mortal man cannot universally and perpetually be head

---

5 Archim. Justin Popović, *Orthodox Church and Ecumenism*, published by
the Holy Monastery of the Archangels Tselie, Valievo of Serbia, page 212.

of this Catholic Church [meaning the Orthodox Church], our Lord Jesus Christ Himself is head, and it is He Himself holding the rudder at the helm in the governing of the Church through the Holy Fathers."[6]

The Synod of the Ecumenical Patriarchate in 1895, under Patriarch Anthimos VII, published an encyclical of exceptional importance to the holy clergy and the pious faithful of the patriarchal throne of Constantinople. It was a response to the encyclical letter of Pope Leo XIII which was addressed to the leaders and the peoples of the world and to the Orthodox Church inviting them to come to the papal Church, thereby recognizing the infallibility, the primacy of authority, and the worldwide authority of the Pope over all the Church. We present the following excerpt:

"The orthodox Eastern and catholic Church of Christ, with the exception of the Son and Word of God, who was ineffably made man, knows no one infallible upon earth. Even the Apostle Peter himself, whose successor the Pope thinks himself to be, thrice denied the Lord, and was twice rebuked by the Apostle Paul, as not walking uprightly according to the truth of the Gospel."[7] While the Orthodox Church preserves the evangelical faith unadulterated, "the present Roman Church is the Church of innovations, of the falsification of the writings of the Church Fathers, and of the misinterpretation of the Holy Scripture and of the decrees of the holy councils, for which she has reasonably and justly been disowned, and is still disowned, so far as she remains in her error. 'For better is a praiseworthy war than a

6 Confession of Dositheus, 1672. Decree 10 <<http://www.crivoice.org/creeddositheus.html>>

7 The Patriarchal Encyclical of 1895 <<http://orthodoxinfo.com/ecumenism/encyc_1895.aspx>>

peace which separates from God,' as Gregory of Nazianzus also says."[8]

At this point I would like to answer a possible objection.

Recently, the Pope and Roman Catholic theologians sometimes speak positively about our Orthodox Church and they engage in demonstrations of good-will toward us. Maybe something has changed which justifies also a change of stance on the part of the Orthodox toward Papism?

Indeed, there are individual Roman Catholics who with honesty express positions sympathetic to the Orthodox.

However, the official line and policy of the Vatican are different. The Vatican employs a kind of bilingualism. When it addresses us, the Vatican uses expressions of love. At other times, and mainly when it addresses Roman Catholics, it employs its older well-known, tough positions. And we ought not forget that every Orthodox-friendly declaration, which does not refer to the Orthodox Church anyway but more generally to the Eastern Church, many Roman Catholics understand as referring to the Uniate communities.

I am referencing a text of the blessed professor of New Testament of the Theological School at the University of Athens, Ioannis Panagopoulos, who could hardly be characterized as an anti-ecumenist, where he is commenting on the encyclical on the unity of the Churches which was addressed 25th May 1995 by Pope John Paul II to the Roman Catholics and all other Christians. It reads:

"To the Orthodox Church [the encyclical] especially devotes enough paragraphs (50-61). While with regard to other Christian communities, it is accepted that they preserve certain authentic elements of Christian truth and holiness (10-13), by contrast, the Orthodox Church is recognized as a sister Church, the other 'lung' of the body of

---

8 Ibid.

Christ (54), which nevertheless is separated from the Roman Catholic Church. Her apostolic succession and Mysteries are recognized as well and her spiritual and liturgical riches are sincerely honored. However, despite this concession, it is clearly implied that the Orthodox Church does not possess the fullness of Christian truth just like the Protestant confessions as long as they do not enter into communion with the Roman See. The Roman Catholic Church wishes to appear once again as source, final authority, and judge of the ecclesiality of all Christian communities. [...] The Encyclical returns with implacability and rigidity to the declarations of the Decree Concerning Ecumenism of the Second Vatican Council. This basic principle is this: 'The communion of all the individual Churches with the Church of Rome: is a necessary presupposition for unity.' The primacy of the bishop of Rome is grounded in the will of God and is understood as oversight (επισκοπή) over ecclesiastical unity, the transmission of the faith, the sacramental and liturgical rites, missionary work, and the canonical order and the Christian life generally. Only communion with the successors of Peter guarantees the fullness of the one, holy, catholic, and apostolic Church. Every conversation about ecclesiastical unity presupposes the acceptance without reservations of the primacy of the Pope which God founded 'as the continual and visible principle and ground of unity.' [...] We Orthodox faithful must confess our thorough disappointment with regards to the new Encyclical of the Pope. Because the traditional Roman Catholic understanding concerning the Church and her unity constituted already from the 5th century the rock of scandal and despite 1500 years of theological dialogues we have not arrived at any positive result and naturally we are not going to have results insofar as the Roman Catholic Church insists intransigently on the claim of papal primacy. [...] It is consequently unforgivable naivety, if one were to claim, that the new Papal Encyclical leaves open the question of primacy. Its only innovation in this question is the reference to the others and the demand in a diplomatic way that all show 'authentic heroism' and 'a sacrifice for unity.'"[9]

This stance of the Vatican and chiefly the unorthodox action of the Unia forced the Ecumenical Patriarchate to interrupt the dialogue with the Roman Catholics. It is also worthy to note that His All-Holiness stated a few months ago to Austrian reporters that apart from the Church of Romania, the Orthodox Churches have not accepted the Balamand agreement.

9 Ioannis Panagopoulos, "The Vatican and the Union of the Christian Churches," newspaper *Kathimerini*, Sunday, 30th July 1995. [Greek] (our own translation).

CHAPTER 5

Anthropocentricism

Between the two Churches there exist other differences such as their teachings concerning the purgatorial fire and their teaching concerning our Panagia which they name Mariology. Declaring as dogma the immaculate conception of the Panagia, they do not understand that with this they separate her from the human race, a fact which has soteriological consequences for humanity: if the Virgin possessed a different nature, then the Lord taking on human nature from her divinized some other nature and not the nature common to all men.

All of these differences have as a common denominator anthropocentrism. A product of anthropocentrism is the forensic and legalistic spirit of Roman Catholicism which appears in the Canon Law and in very many of the institutions of the Western Church.

A simple example which proves the above is the way in which the mystery of Confession happens. The spiritual father and the person confessing enter into two cubicles without seeing each other, and there is conducted a sort of 'trial' in which the person confessing enumerates his sins and he receives the penance which the canons of the Roman Catholic Church define. For the Orthodox Church, this mystery is understood in a completely different manner: there exists an immediate, personal relation between the spiritual father and the person confessing, in which the spiritual father is the father and the person confessing is the spiritual child, a place where he goes to open his heart, to say his pain, his sins, and to receive adequate spiritual healing.

The anthropocentrism of the Roman Catholic Church is apparent also in her continual innovations. On the other hand, the Orthodox Church is un-innovative; she has not added anything to those things which our Lord and His holy Apostles taught. She is the Church which is par excellence evangelical and apostolic, and this is expressed in her life and institutions which are absolutely evangelical and apostolic.

Everything Orthodox is theanthropocentric. In contrast, everything western, either Papist or Protestant, has received more or less the effect of anthropocentrism. For this reason, the blessed Russian theologian and philosopher, Khomiakov, said that Papism and Protestantism are two opposite sides of the same coin.

Saint Nektarios also wrote characteristically comparing the Papal Church with Protestantism: "The only difference between the two systems is the following: In the Papal Church the individual, namely the Pope, gathers around himself many mute and unfree persons compliant to the principles and convictions of the enthroned individual. In Protestantism, the Church is concentrated around the individual. Hence the Papal Church is an individual and nothing more. But who is able to guarantee us the agreement of all the Popes? Since every Pope judges what is upright as he sees fit and interprets the Scripture as he wills, and pontificates as he considers proper, how does this differ from the many pontiffs of the Protestant Church? How do these leaders differ? Equally in the Protestant world each respective individual is a Church, whereas in the Papal Church the entire Church consists of an individual, the particular Pope of each age." The essence is this, the reign of the individual. In Papism the individual Pope reigns, in Protestantism every individual Protestant reigns, and every individual becomes the criterion of truth.

In the Orthodox Church, everything that makes up her life and teaching gives witness to her theanthropocentrism: ecclesiastical art, hagiography, architecture, music, etc. If we compare a Madonna of the Renaissance with a Byzantine Panagia, we will ascertain the difference. The Madonna is a beautiful woman while the Byzantine Panagia is the divinized human being. If we compare St. Peter's Basilica with the Temple of Agia Sofia, we will see how much anthropocentrism is expressed in St. Peter's Basilica where it attempts to impose on the beholder with the weight of the material. On the other hand, entering into Agia Sofia, you feel that you enter into heaven. The temple of Agia Sofia does not try to impress with its riches nor with its materials. The same happens in Byzantine ecclesiastical music as well, which is devotional and leads back to heaven and which does not have any relation with the polyphonic European music which simply gives emotional pleasure to man.

Archimandrite George of Grigoriou

CONCLUSION

For all of these reasons, the union is not a matter of agreement only in some dogmas, but of the reception of the Orthodox, Theanthropocentric, Christocentric, Triadocentric (Trinity-centric) spirit in dogma, in piety, in ecclesiology, in canon law, in pastoral practice, in art, in ascesis.

In order for true union to happen, either we must give up Orthodox theanthropocentrism or the Papists must give their own anthropocentrism. The first can never happen with the Grace of our Lord because this would be betrayal of the Gospel of our Christ. But for the second to happen is difficult. However, "what is impossible for man is possible for God."[1]

We believe that it does not benefit the non-Orthodox for us to renounce our Orthodoxy. As long as there is Orthodoxy, the unchanging evangelical faith is saved, the "faith once delivered to the Saints"[2] It is the living witness of the true communion of God and man; the truth of the Church as theanthropic communion. Thus, even the heterodox who have lost it know that it exists somewhere. They hope. Maybe sometime they will seek it individually or collectively. They will find it and they will find rest. Let us keep this holy faith, not only for us but also for all of our heterodox brothers and for the entire world. The theory of the two lungs, by which the Church breathes, of Papism and

---

1 Luke 18:27.

2 Jude 3.

Orthodoxy, cannot become acceptable from the Orthodox side because the one lung (Papism) does not hold the right faith and indeed it has been stricken incurably ill.

We thank the All-Holy and the Life-giving Trinity for its great gift, our holy Orthodox faith and for our holy ancestors, teachers, priests and bishops, and spiritual fathers who taught us and passed on to us this holy Faith.

We confess that we would not find rest within a Church which in many things substitutes the Theanthropic Christ with an "infallible" man whether he is a "Pope" or a "Protestant."

We believe that our Church is the One, Holy, Catholic, and Apostolic Church of Christ, which has the fullness of Truth and Grace. We are sorry because heterodox Christians cannot bestow this fullness, and indeed sometimes they even try to proselytize Orthodox Christians by luring them into their communities where they have only a partial, fragmentary, and distorted aspect of the truth. We appreciate how much love they have for Christ and the good works which they do, but we cannot accept that the interpretation which they give to the Gospel of Christ is in agreement with the teaching of Christ, of the Holy Apostles, of the holy Fathers and of the Holy Local and Ecumenical Councils.

We pray that the chief shepherd Christ, the only infallible Chief and Head of the Church, will guide them to the Holy Orthodox Church which is their paternal house from which they have fallen away, and that he may enlighten us Orthodox Christians to remain until death faithful to our holy and unchanging Faith made more and more strong and delving ever deeper "until we all attain to the unity of the faith and of the knowledge of the Son of God, to mature manhood, to the measure of the stature of the fullness of Christ."[3] Amen.

---

3 Ephesians 4:13.

UNCUT MOUNTAIN PRESS TITLES

Books by Archpriest Peter Heers

Fr. Peter Heers, *The Ecclesiological Renovation of Vatican II: An Orthodox Examination of Rome's Ecumenical Theology Regarding Baptism and the Church*, 2015

Fr. Peter Heers, *The Missionary Origins of Modern Ecumenism: Milestones Leading up to 1920*, 2007

The Works of our Father Among the Saints, Nikodemos the Hagiorite

Vol. 1: *Exomologetarion: A Manual of Confession*

Vol. 2: *Concerning Frequent Communion of the Immaculate Mysteries of Christ*

Vol. 3: *Confession of Faith*

Other Available Titles

Elder Cleopa of Romania, *The Truth of our Faith, Vol. I: Discourses from Holy Scripture on the Tenants of Christian Orthodoxy*

Elder Cleopa of Romania, *The Truth of our Faith, Vol. II: Discourses from Holy Scripture on the Holy Mysteries*

Fr. John Romanides, *Patristic Theology: The University Lectures of Fr. John Romanides*

Demetrios Aslanidis and Monk Damascene Grigoriatis, *Apostle to Zaire: The Life and Legacy of Blessed Father Cosmas of Grigoriou*

Protopresbyter Anastasios Gotsopoulos, *On Common Prayer with the Heterodox According to the Canons of the Church*

Robert Spencer, *The Church and the Pope*

G. M. Davis, *Antichrist: The Fulfillment of Globalization*

Athonite Fathers of the 20th Century, Vol. I

St. Gregory Palamas, *Apodictic Treatises on the Procession of the Holy Spirit*

St. Hilarion Troitsky, *On the Dogma of the Church: An Historical Overview of the Sources of Ecclesiology*

Fr. Alexander Webster and Fr. Peter Heers, Editors, *Let No One Fear Death*

Subdeacon Nektarios Harrison, *Metropolitan Philaret of New York: Zealous Confessor for the Faith*

Archimandrite Ephraim Triandaphillopoulos, *Noetic Prayer as the Basis of Mission and the Struggle Against Heresy*

Select Forthcoming Titles

Nicholas Baldimtsis, *Life and Witness of St. Iakovos of Evia*

Georgio, *Errors of the Latins*

Fr. Peter Heers, *Going Deeper in the Spiritual Life*

Abbe Guette, *The Papacy*

Athonite Fathers of the 20th Century, Vol. II

This 1ˢᵗ Edition of

Catholicism in Light of Orthodoxy

written by Archimandrite George, translated by Vincent DeWeese, edited by Karen Evans, with cover design by George Weis, and typeset in Baskerville in this two thousand and twenty second year of our Lord's Holy Incarnation is one of the many fine titles available from Uncut Mountain Press, translators and publishers of Orthodox Christian theological and spiritual literature. Find the book you are looking for at

u n c u t m o u n t a i n p r e s s . c o m

**GLORY BE TO GOD
FOR ALL THINGS**

AMEN.

Made in the USA
Las Vegas, NV
26 October 2024

10513396R00025